Anonymous

Semi-Centennial Celebration of the Franklin Fire Insurance Company of Philadelphia

June 25, 1879

Anonymous

Semi-Centennial Celebration of the Franklin Fire Insurance Company of Philadelphia
June 25, 1879

ISBN/EAN: 9783337250485

Printed in Europe, USA, Canada, Australia, Japan

Cover: Foto ©ninafisch / pixelio.de

More available books at **www.hansebooks.com**

SEMI-CENTENNIAL CELEBRATION

OF THE

FRANKLIN FIRE INSURANCE COMPANY

OF

PHILADELPHIA.

SEMI-CENTENNIAL

CELEBRATION

OF THE

FRANKLIN FIRE INSURANCE COMPANY

OF

PHILADELPHIA.

JUNE 25, 1879.

PUBLISHED BY REQUEST.

PHILADELPHIA,
1879.

SEMI-CENTENNIAL CELEBRATION.

EXTRACT from the Minutes of a meeting of the Board of Directors of the Franklin Fire Insurance Company of Philadelphia, held March 5, 1879:

"On motion of Mr. R. D. Benson, the following Resolution was adopted :

"*Resolved*, That a Committee of *two* be appointed, who, with the President and Vice-President, shall be authorized to take action for the proper commemoration of the Semi-Centennial of this Company, June 25th next; also that the President be requested to prepare and deliver an address appropriate to such an event.

"The President appointed Messrs. R. D. Benson and F. P. Steel, Committee."

In pursuance of the arrangements perfected by the committee, the following-named gentlemen met together at Augustin's, 1105 Walnut Street, on June 25, 1879 :

OFFICERS.

ALFRED G. BAKER, President.

JAS. W. MCALLISTER, Vice-President.

EZRA T. CRESSON, Secretary.

SAMUEL W. KAY, Assistant Secretary.

Directors.

ALFRED FITLER,
WM. S. GRANT,
THOMAS S. ELLIS,
GUSTAVUS S. BENSON,
R. DALE BENSON,
FRANCIS P. STEEL,
THOMPSON DERR.

A. C. BLODGET, General Agent.

GEO. F. REGER, Manager Department of the East and South.

CHAS. W. KELLOGG, Manager Department of the West.

And the following invited guests :

HON. HENRY C. CAREY.

CHARLES DUTILH.

GEORGE W. BIDDLE, Counsel of the Company.

CHAS. J. MARTIN, President Home Insurance Company of New York.

JAS. SOMERS SMITH, Secretary and Treasurer Philadelphia Contributionship.

HENRY D. SHERRERD, President Insurance Company of the State of Pennsylvania.

RICHARD S. SMITH, President Union Insurance Company.

JAMES W. COCHRAN, Lexington, Kentucky.

JAMES G. COFFIN, Pittsburgh, Pennsylvania.

D. B. CUMMINS, President Girard National Bank.

WM. L. SCHAFFER, Cashier Girard National Bank.

JAMES L. CLAGHORN, President Commercial National Bank.

E. P. GRAHAM, Cashier Commercial National Bank.

S. W. BELL, Cashier Farmers' and Mechanics' National Bank.

PETER LAMB, Cashier Southwark National Bank.

GEO. FALES BAKER.

E. ALEX. SCOTT.

After the removal of the cloth the President arose and said:

THE PRESIDENT: Here are some letters of regret which will now be read. This one is from Isaac Lea, our Senior Director. I visited him at Long Branch on Saturday last, and found him sitting on his porch, nigh unto the seashore, hale, healthy, and hearty. He stated that he was very sorry he could not be with us, but appreciated everything that was being done to celebrate the semi-centennial anniversary of the company.

LONG BRANCH, N. J.,
June 18, 1879.

MY DEAR SIR,—I have received the invitation to be present at the Semi-Centennial Celebration of the "Franklin Fire Insurance Company of Philadelphia," and greatly regret that it is entirely out of my power to accept it.

I am perfectly aware how much the stockholders are indebted to their late President, Chas. N. Bancker, Esq., for its foundation, as well as for its pre-eminent prosperity. I knew Mr. Bancker in my early youth, when he was the largest importer of merchandise in the United States,—about 1808. Subsequently he was brought down by the speculations of others. With his former energy and intelligence, in 1829 he established on a sure foundation the Franklin Fire Insurance Company, the present status of which needs nothing to be said. His friends made up the subscription. Subsequent to organization I made frequent purchases until I became one of the largest stockholders interested.

In 1852, while I was in Europe, I was elected to the Board of Directors, and I am now the oldest member of it.

Mr. Bancker's old friends well remember how much he was

interested in natural philosophy and astronomy, and what superior instruments he possessed in these branches of knowledge, as well also with what liberality he then gave to younger men like myself the use of them.

In the sudden death of our President, Mr. Bancker, you will remember what perplexity we were in as directors, and I may now, I think, congratulate the stockholders, and take some credit to myself, as chairman of the committee, when I asked you to take that responsible position in which over three millions were intrusted to us. It was unexpected to you, and you hesitated, but fortunately for the stockholders you acceded to the wishes of the Directors, and the Company is now foremost in the rank of insurers, known over the whole country for its absolute security and promptness. Continuing under your charge, I have no doubt this prosperity will be permanent.

Very resp'y yours, etc.,

ISAAC LEA.

A. G. BAKER, ESQ.,
  President Franklin Fire Insurance Company.

Mr. Lea's sentences are rather too complimentary to myself.

The next letter is from Caleb Cope, President of the old Philadelphia Saving-Fund, and I will preface the reading of it by saying that we regret his absence, inasmuch as that staunch corporation, organized in 1809, had for one of its originators the late Charles N. Bancker, while Mr. Bancker also laid the corner-stone of their new building, corner of Seventh and Walnut Streets. The seal of the Saving-Fund bears the image of FRANKLIN.

To the President and Directors of the Franklin Fire Insurance Company of Philadelphia:

Gentlemen,—I feel honored by your invitation to dine with you on the occasion of your commemorating the Semi-Centennial anniversary of your prosperous institution.

I regret, however, to add that, governed by a rule imposed by infirmities incident to old age, I have long since refrained from meeting my friends in social assemblages, and accordingly must deny myself the pleasure which I would otherwise enjoy in being present at so interesting a period as the one alluded to.

With cordial thanks for the compliment tendered me, and my fervent good wishes in behalf of the institution you represent, and yourselves individually,

I am very respectfully yours,

C. COPE.

Philada., June 14th, '79.

Our senior counsel, Eli K. Price, Esq., who, on the occasion of all our usual festivities, has had his place at this table, rather surprised us yesterday by sending a regret. We had hoped that he would have been present at this time.

709 Walnut Street,

June 24th, 1879.

My Dear Sir,—I thank you for your kind invitation to your festive commemorative gathering. It will afford you occasion to state what has been your aggregate success after having fully met the losses of your customers according to your obligation. May your company ever thus be able to exhibit its strength after full performance of its most important duty of protecting others from loss !

2

I wish my absence not to be taken as the slightest reflection upon those that partake the pleasures of the festive board. It is yet the right of my juniors to enjoy the good things a kind Providence has provided for them. All I ask is that they will kindly remember and excuse the more than octogenarian, who remembers with pleasure many such annual meetings. These were occasions of exchanging much valuable information, and enabled all the participants to know and appreciate each other better. An eminent English judge said that they " were great lubricators of business." He no doubt meant that they increased good-will among men and the trust man may safely place in man. Yet the old man of eighty-two asks excuse. As to him, " the custom is more honored in the breach than in the observance." The health and strength God gives, it is his duty to carefully husband, that he may make the most enduring use of the life and faculties given, and yet longer discharge the duty of trying to be useful to society and to live in the love of his fellow-beings.

Though not personally with you, I approve, and in feeling shall be with you, and am

Your friend, and friend of you all,

ELI K. PRICE.

ALFRED G. BAKER, ESQ.

It was the intent of the Directors, and the invitations were so sent out, that the Presidents of all companies that antedated the Franklin in organization should sit with us to-day. J. Somers Smith is here, representing the old Contributionship. David Lewis sends his regrets,—the Mutual Assurance of 1784. Charles Platt, of the Insurance Company of North America, 1794, sends his regrets, but with them an appropriate toast: " May they live long and prosper!" The State of Pennsylvania of the same year is here in the person of its President, Henry D. Sherrerd. We then come to the Union, 1804, represented by Richard S. Smith, President, now in his ninetieth year,—ninety years old in August next! I have his letter of acceptance. The handwriting is so remarkable that I propose to keep it as a memento. He may smile as we look at him, but I know it is a wonderful piece of paper. Then here is a letter from Thos. R. Maris, of the American Fire, 1810, regretting that he cannot be with us. I received a letter of acceptance from A. Loudon Snowden, of the Fire Association, 1820, but for some reason he is not here.* Also one of regret from John Devereux, President Pennsylvania Fire, 1825.

---

* Mr. Snowden was taken suddenly sick at the Mint during the afternoon, requiring medical attendance on getting to his residence; an enforced absence, which caused him much annoyance, as his note subsequently advised us.

ADDRESS.

Fellow Directors, Associate Officers, and Friends:

Fifty years old! We have met in this room to-day to do honor to the Franklin Fire Insurance Company of Philadelphia; to celebrate in a proper way the semi-centennial of this corporation. At the request of the Board of Directors, the pleasing duty of speaking some facts that surround its life up to the present hour has been placed upon its President.

Fifty years old! In one sense, that period may not seem so long, yet when it bears upon a corporation, and one that has for its 'sphere the precarious business of Fire Insurance, the years are many in number. They tell of trials and losses, they speak of experience dearly bought, they become a beacon to those about entering upon the same treacherous sea that has wrecked so many well-trimmed vessels, and has caused so much capital to melt away like snow under an April sun. As we linger over the doings and events about to be given, let us divest our minds altogether of the idea so current nowadays, that the Fire Insurance business is one of "luck" solely; it is a false doctrine which time has set aside. Care, close attention to detail, application, along with the study of statistics, all do their special share in making any institution a success; without them underwriting, as any other business, only leads to loss and ruin. "CHANCE" had nothing to do with the past history of this Company. "HAPHAZARD" can claim no credit for elevating it to the high position it now holds among the people.

FIFTY YEARS OLD! Dwelling upon this simple though pleasing thought and its surrounding reflections, the sketch of the "Franklin's" life now begins.

The charter of the company, perpetual in its provisions, was obtained from the Legislature in 1829. It was approved by Governor J. Andrew Shulze, April 22d of that year. The commissioners for receiving subscriptions to the stock were Charles Graff, Benjamin W. Richards, John K. Kane, Robert Toland, Levi Ellmaker, Robert Taylor, James Schott, Peter Hertzog, Thomas Cave, Charles N. Bancker, Samuel Patton, and Robert O'Neil. These men are now all dead. Pursuant to notice in the public newspapers of the day, the books were opened May 13th, at the house of Daniel Rubicam, No. 20 South Sixth Street, and were closed upon the following day, the stock having been all subscribed. Shortly after, an advertisement in the daily newspapers appeared, signed by all the commissioners, stating the fact; also calling a meeting of the stockholders to elect directors, June 8th, from 10 A.M. to 1 P.M., at the same place. The first meeting was held that day. Richard Willing was made president, and Charles Dutilh was selected to act as secretary.

John K. Kane made the report of the commissioners that the stock had been subscribed in conformity with the Act of Assembly, and the proper authorities legally notified of the same. Thomas I. Wharton moved that the charter as now read be received and accepted. Carried. Erskine Hazard, William Kirkham, and Robert O'Neil were appointed judges of election. When the polls closed the following-named shareholders were declared elected :

Richard Willing,

James Schott,

Samuel W. Jones,

Thomas Hart,

Henry C. Carey,

Thomas I. Wharton,

Tobias Wagner,

Charles Roberts,

Levi Ellmaker,

William Chaloner.

The following-named persons have filled the varied official positions, following each other in order of succession as read :

ELECTION.	NAME.	REMARKS.
	PRESIDENTS.	
June, 1829.	Samuel W. Jones.	Declined to serve, June, 1829. Now deceased.
June, 1829.	Richard Willing.	Declined a re-election, Oct. 1829. Now deceased.
Oct. 1829.	William Chaloner.	Declined to serve, Oct. 1829. Now deceased.
Dec. 1829.	Clement C. Biddle.	Declined a re-election, Oct. 1834. Now deceased.
Oct. 1834.	Henry C. Carey.	Resigned, Feb. 1837.
Feb. 1837.	Charles N. Bancker.	Deceased, Feb. 1869.
Feb. 1869.	*Alfred G. Baker.*	Now in office.
	VICE-PRESIDENTS.	
Oct. 1857.	Edward C. Dale.	Deceased, Dec. 1866.
Jan. 1867.	George Fales.	Deceased, Jan. 1879.
Dec. 1871.	Jas. W. McAllister, 2d.	Elected Vice-President, Feb. 1879.
Feb. 1879.	*Jas. W. McAllister.*	Now in office.
	SECRETARIES.	
June, 1829.	Charles N. Bancker.	Elected President, Feb. 1837. Now deceased.
Feb. 1837.	Charles G. Bancker.	Resigned, March, 1857. Now deceased.
March, 1857.	Peter Notman.	Declined to serve, March, 1857.
April, 1857.	Wm. A. Steel, Sec. pro-tem.	Deceased, April, 1861.
April, 1861.	J. W. McAllister, Sec. pro-tem.	Elected Secretary, Feb. 1869.
Feb. 1869.	Jas. W. McAllister.	Elected Director and 2d Vice-President, Dec. 1871.
Dec. 1871.	Theodore M. Reger.	Resigned, Oct. 1878.
Oct. 1878.	*Ezra T. Cresson.*	Now in office.
	ASSISTANT SECRETARIES.	
June, 1868.	William Green.	Resigned, May, 1869.
May, 1869.	Theodore M. Reger.	Elected Secretary, Dec. 1871.
Dec. 1871.	*Samuel W. Kay.*	Now in office.
	GENERAL AGENT.	
May, 1873.	*Amos C. Blodget.*	Now in office.

The company began business June 25, 1829, at No. 163½ Chestnut Street, under a lease from Stephen Girard, duly signed by himself. In October, 1844, from the demands of an increasing business, No. 163, an adjoining property, was rented also. Under the new numbering ordered by the City Councils these buildings became Nos. 435 and 437. The rental in 1849 was $2400 per annum, which, through various renewals, increased in 1870 to $6000 for twelve months. Upon May 1, 1873, the " Franklin" moved to its present locality, No. 421 Walnut Street, which had been bought by the directors, and the building adapted to the growing wants of the company.

The first perpetual policy was issued as follows :

"No. 1. Issued July 20, 1829, to ALEXANDER HENRY. Transferred December, 1845, to SUSAN M. JACKSON, and again to OLIVER EVANS, present owner, October, 1856, covering a three-story brick building, situate No. 65 North Second Street, now occupied as a picture-frame manufactory. $2000 at 3 per cent. deposit."

This policy is still in force as originally issued, but afterwards increased to cover a greater hazard, the owner being the same OLIVER EVANS.

The following is a copy of the order for the first temporary insurance :

1829. July 21.	✓ 1.	*To the Franklin Fire Insurance Company of Philada: Make insurance for the space of* Four months *against loss or damage by fire on* Seven unfinished Four Story Brick Houses, situated on the South West corner of Fourth and Walnut Streets, upon which property Five thousand dollars are already insured at the office of the Pennsylvania Fire Insurance Company.

Sum to be insured, Dollars 5000, @ 30
cts. p. 100$ . . . . 15 Dolls.
=Policy . . 1=

Novr. 21,   =Ds. 16=
1829.
            MATHEW CAREY,
                  pr H. C. CAREY.

It is a matter of much regret this policy cannot be found. Numbers two and three were issued to the firm of CAREY, LEA & CAREY, the orders being signed in the handwriting of HENRY C. CAREY, ESQ. ISAAC LEA, ESQ., our senior director, still living, now in his eighty-eighth year, was a member of that firm.

Among those who were original stockholders we find the following names, well-known citizens, who, during their day and generation, held a high position among their fellow-men :

Richard Ashhurst,	Thomas Hart,
Chas. N. Bancker,	Erskine Hazard,
Clement C. Biddle,	Peter Hertzog,
Wm. A. Blanchard,	John K. Kane,
J. J. Borie,	William Kirkham,
Frederick Brown,	James Latimer,
John Rea Barton,	John McAllister, Jr.,
John Cadwallader,	Samuel Patton,
Henry Chancellor,	William Rawle,
Nathaniel Chapman,	Benjamin W. Richards,
Elihu Chauncey,	James Schott,
Edward C. Dale,	Robert Taylor,
Geo. Fales,	Robert Toland,
Coleman Fisher,	Tobias Wagner,
Charles Graff,	Thos. I. Wharton,
Samuel Grant,	Richard Willing.

Three of those who were shareholders at the birth of this corporation still live, viz. :

Henry C. Carey,
Arthur G. Coffin,
Charles Dutilh.

Two of them, Messrs. Carey and Dutilh, time-honored Philadelphians, unite with us in our celebration. We regret the enforced absence of Mr. Arthur G. Coffin, for so many years the widely-respected President of the Insurance Company of North America. The infirmities of advanced life are a bar to his presence. We can well assert he is in full harmony with all that is said and done by us, who know him as a "friend to the Franklin" in every sense of the word. Mr. Carey was an original director, as you have heard, while he is also the only living ex-president whom we can honor. Mr. Charles Dutilh was secretary of the gathering of the stockholders having for its purpose the acceptance of the charter as well as the election of the first board of directors.

So few out of so many! The tale of five times ten years carries along with it food for serious thought and solemn study.

Since organization, forty stockholders have at different times been members of the Board of Directors. The roll is herewith given :

NO.	DATE.	NAME.	REMARKS.	SUCCESSOR
1	June, 1829.	Richard Willing.	Retired, Oct. 1829.	Samuel Grant.
2	"	James Schott.	Retired, Oct. 1842.	David S. Brown.
3	"	Samuel W. Jones.	Retired, Oct. 1829.	William Kirkham.
4	"	Thomas Hart.	Retired, Oct. 1852.	Isaac Lea.
5	"	Henry C. Carey.	Resigned, Feb. 1837.	Chas. N. Bancker.
6	"	Thos. I. Wharton.	Resigned, Nov. 1845.	Morris Patterson.
7	"	Tobias Wagner.	Deceased, ? 1868.	Alfred G. Baker.
8	"	Charles Roberts.	Retired, Oct. 1830.	Richard Ashhurst.
9	"	Levi Ellmaker.	Deceased, April, 1835.	William Chaloner.
10	"	William Chaloner.	Resigned, Sept. 1832.	Frederick Brown.
11	Oct. 1829.	Samuel Grant.	Deceased, Sept. 1872.	J. W. McAllister.
12	"	William Kirkham.	Resigned, Oct. 1829.	Clement C. Biddle.
13	Dec. 1829.	Clement C. Biddle.	Retired, Oct. 1837.	Geo. W. Richards.
14	Oct. 1830.	Richard Ashhurst.	Resigned, Nov. 1830.	T. C. Rockhill.
15	Nov. 1830.	T. C. Rockhill.	Retired, Oct. 1837.	Jacob R. Smith.
16	Sept. 1832.	Frederick Brown.	Resigned, Sept. 1871.	A. E. Borie.
17	May, 1835.	William Chaloner.	Retired, Oct. 1838.	M. D. Lewis.
18	Feb. 1837.	Chas. N. Bancker.	Deceased, Feb. 1869.	Gust. S. Benson.
19	Oct. 1837.	Geo. W. Richards.	Deceased, April, 1874.	R. Dale Benson.
20	"	Jacob R. Smith.	Deceased, ? 1865.	Peter McCall.
21	Oct. 1838.	M. D. Lewis.	Deceased, Feb. 1861.	Alfred Fitler.
22	Oct. 1841.	A. E. Borie.	Resigned, Oct. 1856.	George Fales.
23	Oct. 1842.	David S. Brown.	Resigned, Jan. 1864.	Fras. W. Lewis.
24	April, 1846.	Morris Patterson.	Retired, Oct. 1855.	Edward C. Dale.
25	Oct. 1852.	Isaac Lea.	Now Senior Director.	
26	Oct. 1855.	Edward C. Dale.	Deceased, Dec. 1866.	Wm. A. Blanchard.
27	Oct. 1856.	George Fales.	Deceased, Jan. 1879.	Thompson Derr.
28	Oct. 1861.	Alfred Fitler.	Now a member.	
29	Jan. 1864.	Fras. W. Lewis.	Resigned, Jan. 1869.	Thomas S. Ellis.
30	Oct. 1865.	Peter McCall.	Retired, Oct. 1867.	William S. Grant.
31	Jan. 1867.	Wm. A. Blanchard.	Declined to serve.	Thomas Sparks.
32	Feb. 1867.	Thomas Sparks.	Deceased, Oct. 1874.	Francis P. Steel.
33	Oct. 1867.	William S. Grant.	Now a member.	
34	Oct. 1868.	Alfred G. Baker.	" " "	
35	Jan. 1869.	Thomas S. Ellis.	" " "	
36	Feb. 1869.	Gust. S. Benson.	" " "	
37	Oct. 1872.	J. W. McAllister.	" " "	
38	July, 1874.	R. Dale Benson.	" " "	
39	Nov. 1874.	Francis P. Steel.	" " "	
40	Feb. 1879.	Thompson Derr.	" " "	

As a connecting link between 1829 and 1879, the colored porter, Mingo Ricks, still lives in good health,

doing his work every day. One of the earliest entries
in the Cash-Book of 1829 reads as follows:

"Paid Mingo Ricks for services . . . $5.00."

His heart has been gladdened this day by a gift from
the Company appropriate to a term of service covering
half a century, during all of which time Mingo has been
truthful, faithful, and honest.

The synopsis of the dividends declared is now pre-
sented as a matter of special interest :

NOS.	DATES.	PER CENT.	NOS.	DATES.	PER CENT.
1	Sept. 1831.	3	42–43	1853.	12
2	1832.	4	44–47	1854–1855.	18
3–14	1833–1838.	8	48–49	1856.	22
15–18	1839–1840.	9	50–51	1857.	24
19–30	1841–1846.	10	52–53	1858.	30
31–32	1847.	11	54–73	1859–1868.	32
33–34	1848.	12	74–75	1869.	34
35–36	1849.	16	76–77	1870.	35
37–38	1850.	12	78–110	1871–1879.	32
39–40	1851.	10			
41	1852.	6		Average,	20

Gold dividends began with No. 78, April, 1871.
"   "   ceased with No. 105, January, 1878.
Whole amount paid since 1831, $3,767,016.

From this summary we learn that during each year
since 1831 the "Franklin," without a single exception,
has paid an annual dividend, the yearly average during
that time being TWENTY PER CENT. It is doubted if

there exists a corporation anywhere that can make such an exhibit. It shows the wisdom of a moderate capital, supplemented by a large surplus, carefully guarded by the directors to meet heavy losses when they every now and then occur.

It is a matter worthy of note to relate the large fires in Philadelphia in which the Company paid over $25,000.

DATE.	LOCALITY, ETC.	LOSS PAID.
May 21, 1836.	Front Street below Chestnut. Stores.	$34,428.95
Oct. 4, 1839.	Front and Chestnut Streets. Stores.	44,955.37
July 9, 1850.	The " Great Fire," originating in Brock's stores, in Water Street near Callowhill. 300 buildings destroyed. Loss, $1,500,000.	94,123.96
Dec. 27, 1851.	N. E. cor. of Sixth and Chestnut Streets. Stores.	29,226.08
March 28, 1852.	Strawberry and Bank Streets. Stores.	78,453.94
July 5, 1854.	Ninth and Chestnut Streets. National Theatre, Chinese Museum, stores, etc.	27,789.06
Dec. 14, 1854.	N. W. cor. of Fifth and Chestnut Streets. Stores.	53,699.45
April 11, 1856.	Ranstead Place, between Fourth and Fifth Streets, above Chestnut. Stores.	31,964.97
May 1, 1856.	Sixth and Chestnut Streets. Stores.	60,480.09

From this tabulation we find that at various dates the " Franklin" has paid large sums to those of this city who held her policies, in the highest confidence, as indemnity against loss from fire.

The results of the business during half a century are now in order.   The records are as follows:

| Perpetual deposit premiums received | . | . $2,603,481.64 |
| Losses paid on perpetuals | . . . | . 1,055,863.38 |

	TEMPORARY PREMIUMS.	LOSSES PAID.
Home . .	$4,484,177.35	$2,671,490.15
Agency	12,850,773.32	7,361,483.70

Net gain in agency over and above all losses paid and expenses: $1,002,366.48, or 7¾ per cent., including losses by great fires at Chicago, in 1871 ($635,429.39); Boston, in 1872 ($451,504.97); St. Louis, in 1849 ($294,855.42); and Pittsburgh, in 1845.($19,936).

In placing before you this abstract, one thing must not be lost sight of: the percentage of profit does NOT include any gain arising from the custody of the money, which is a very large item of profit, accruing during a series of years.

The first agency planted by the "Franklin" was at Lexington, Kentucky, in 1831. At that early date the method was crude; to this Company must be given the crown of being the pioneer in a.system of business that has grown with the growth of this land to one of vast proportions. She might be named as the "van-courier" in the agency field. John Tilford, a merchant of the town, was duly appointed. Jas. W. Cochran, who is present with us to-day, was a boy in his employ, who used to pass some of his evenings in writing up surveys for the risks taken. This same boy has grown to manhood, and still in his more matured years retains the agency in a city which, under his care and conservative manner of business, has shown a wonderful record:

Since 1831 the receipts have been   . $173,390.68
Losses and expenditures .   .   .   108,894.36
                                      _____
  Net profit . $64,496.32   37$\frac{20}{}$ per cent.

This worthy representative bears the honored title of being the "SENIOR AGENT OF THE FRANKLIN." The late president, Charles N. Bancker, Esq., developed this new plan of increasing the moneyed returns by following up Lexington with agencies at Trenton, York, Newark, Richmond, Nashville, Baltimore, Pittsburgh, and at many other points. At each of these cities the Company has its representatives this very day in good working order.

We now pass to the agency at Pittsburgh. Our respected friend, James G. Coffin, who also unites in these festivities, and graces our table with himself in person, was appointed agent in 1849, having therefore been in active service thirty years. No man in the employ of this institution carries with him a higher record for integrity and prudent management than him to whom we now award such words of praise. May he live long to be known as "OUR ESTEEMED PITTSBURGH AGENT." The figures of that city tell their own well-marked tale:

Receipts since 1844 .   .   .   . $711,720.69
Losses and expenditures .   .   .   353,214.44
                                      _____
                                       $358,506.25   50$\frac{37}{}$ per cent.

This includes the losses by the big fire in 1845.

The Company has had two representatives in New
York City, who have both kindly responded to the invitation to unite in this celebration; we greet their coming
to partake of our hospitalities with a hearty welcome.
The president of the Home Insurance Company of New
York, Charles J. Martin, Esq., and the vice-president of
the Niagara Insurance Company, of the same city, Peter
Notman, Esq., are also in our midst.* These eminently
successful men in their present walks of life once had
charge of our office in New York City. The former-
named gentleman presents to us the following figures, in
evidence of his well-conducted administration, viz.:

1849 and 1850. Receipts   .   . $49,782.61
Losses and expenditures .   .   .   24,596.63

    Net profit .   . $25,185.98   50⁸⁰/₁₀ per cent.

Mr. Martin left the service of the Company to become
interested in that wonderfully successful corporation of
which he is now the respected president, to be followed
by Peter Notman, Esq., who discharged the duties of the
position from 1850 to 1858, extending over about eight
years. To cover this period, the following figures are
submitted:

1850 @ 1858. Receipts .   . $305,027.34
Losses and expenditures .   .   201,556.31

    Net profit .   .   .   . $103,471.03   33¹⁸/₁₀ per cent.

---

* For some unexplained reason Mr. Notman's chair was vacant during
the whole evening. No word has ever been received from him.

4

Mr. Notman was elected secretary by the directors in 1857, but declined to serve, shortly afterwards becoming connected with the Niagara Insurance Company.

Such results speak for themselves. We congratulate ourselves that such careful, prudent underwriters are near to us at this hour; we tender to them thanks for what they have done for the " Franklin ;" we can offer to them no higher eulogium than to say to them, merged in a few little words, as a unit of praise,—

"YOU HAVE DONE YOUR DUTY."

EASTVILLE, VIRGINIA. This agency must be named as being a "FIRST HONOR." It was opened in 1839, forty years ago. Premiums were taken during each and every year up to this very week. The only outlays have been the usual charges for commissions, taxes, etc. Not a single cent has ever been claimed or paid for losses. The net profit to the credit of Eastville, Virginia, on the books is $16,309.15,—ONE HUNDRED PER CENT.!!

We doubt if any other company can present such an abstract of business covering forty years at any single agency.

IN MEMORIAM.

It is fitting we should now pause to pay tribute to the memory of three men who were closely connected with the interests of the " Franklin" from its very start. Reference is had to

CHARLES N. BANCKER,

GEORGE FALES,

SAMUEL GRANT,

a Trinomial Group, than which it is hardly likely its equal can be found anywhere else. During more than three-score years they were intimately associated in their business relations, while they lived almost as "THREE IN ONE" as to this Company. May we now call to mind how much it owes to their steady determination and to their skilled experience for its past record, for its present strength!

CHARLES N. BANCKER. My venerable predecessor first conceived the idea of the formation of this Insurance Institution, worked with zeal to get the charter (no common labor even in those days), and in the end saw his exertions crowned with success, when the office was ready for business this very day Fifty years ago. Through years of gain and loss, of hope and despondency, he lived until February 16, 1869, dying then, while still its President, in the ninety-second year of his age.

GEORGE FALES. The late highly-esteemed Vice-President was a subscriber to the stock, when the books were first opened, for fifty shares. Everything in and around the "Franklin" was to him a matter of the greatest interest; he was steady to all its calls during his Directorship. He was the last living stockholder who had never sold a single share during nearly half a century; his estate at this hour owns the original certificate. He held his official position at the request of the Board until he passed away from earth, January 14, 1879, in the ninety-second year of his age.

SAMUEL GRANT. A shareholder at the birth of the Company, as well as a Director in continuous service from October, 1829, until the date of his death, his aim was solely to advance the interests of this Corporation in all ways honorable and just. A prominent and successful merchant, and a highly-respected citizen of Philadelphia, he died September 23, 1872, in the ninetieth year of his age.

As the memory of this remarkable Trio of Men, who all lived to be nonagenarians, is brought before us to dwell upon, and as the recollections of bygone days are recalled by those now living, let us hope that the same wise counsels may ever prevail in the future management that they gave to it in the past; that their acts, energy, and experience may through all time be as guide-posts to us and to those who come after us.

The mortal remains of Charles N. Bancker rest in the same churchyard within a few hundred feet of those of Benjamin Franklin; while the graves of Samuel Grant and George Fales are to be found near unto one another in their adjoining burial-lots at Laurel Hill Cemetery.

> "For we are the same our Fathers have been;
> We see the same sights our Fathers have seen;
> We drink the same stream, we view the same sun,
> And run the same course our Fathers have run.

"The thoughts we are thinking our Fathers would think;
From the death we are shrinking our Fathers would shrink;
To the life we are clinging they also would cling,
But it speeds for us all, like a bird on the wing.

"They died, aye! they died, and we things that are now,
Who walk on the turf that lies over their brow,
Who make in their dwellings a transient abode,
Meet the things that they met on their pilgrimage road."

The history of Fifty years has been spoken, the story's told!

Let me add that it is but human to feel an inward pride in being the head executive of such a corporation. The happy surroundings of the present moment, this hour of good cheer, joined with the reminiscences of the past that have been brought before us, all breathe musical. My own term of office as President covers more than a decade of years. It is a proper wish to bear testimony just here to the kind assistance the Directors, other officers, and employees have at all times given any suggestions and efforts on my own part to advance the "Franklin" still farther in her onward march. To no single man should the credit be given of doing what has been done: we are all component parts of the "Great Unit" which has for its aim the carrying on of the business with safety to both the policy-holders, who look for indemnity in the hour of disaster, and to the share-holders, who expect their regular quarterly income. Any seeming egotism is now pardonable if a few words of kind advice are now spoken to him who may stand in this place, and who may say a few words to those who gather together to do honor to the " Franklin," to drink a toast to her continued prosperity, it may be ten, twenty, or fifty years hence! Let him consider well that no calling in life can be a success unless all interested in it work for the common good; time, labor, thought, and brain-culture must be given freely, at all times tempered with experience, while he must be ever ready to grapple with each new phase of the business that may from time to time present itself. To use a trite expression, "*His heart must be in it.*"

May my successor, and those who follow him, be inspirited with principles like those, which have often-times cheered him who now utters them! All that is within me responds to those truths, to this gathering of friends around the festive table, to this most auspicious hour. Dear old company, I do love thee! " *All earth shall never pluck thee from my heart:* thy history is engraved upon my memory in footprints that will endure until death does us part. *Who, who shall proclaim divorce between thee and me ?*" Let us now accord unto thee an emblematic device taken from Holy Writ, and thereby liken thee unto "A WISE MAN WHO BUILT HIS HOUSE UPON A ROCK:

"AND THE RAIN DESCENDED, AND THE FLOODS CAME, AND THE WINDS BLEW, AND BEAT UPON THAT HOUSE; AND IT FELL NOT: FOR IT WAS FOUNDED UPON A ROCK."

The reading of the Address called forth from those present hearty and generous applause.

THE PRESIDENT: The first regular toast is

"BYGONE DAYS. WHILE IT IS SWEET TO CALL UP BEFORE US THEIR MEMORY, SUCH THOUGHTS ARE INTERMINGLED WITH SORROW THAT MANY WE ONCE KNEW SO WELL ARE AWAY IN THEIR DWELLINGS OF REST,"

which will be responded to by Mr. Henry C. Carey, former President of the Company. (Applause.)

HON. HENRY C. CAREY.

Mr. President,—Your toast covers for some of us, my friend here (Mr. Richard S. Smith) and myself particularly, a broad expanse of time. It carries me back to ·the time when, eighty years ago, I witnessed the funeral ceremonies of the then just deceased grandest man of ancient or modern times,—our Washington !

A little later I see myself part of an assemblage in the House of Representatives, in June, 1812, listening to Mr. Clay and other great men of the time, all of whom have since passed away, engaged in discussing the question of war with Britain. Still later, I see my friend Baneker struggling day after day and month after month against the most serious opposition in his efforts to obtain the charter of your Company. So serious was the opposition that at times he was disposed to give it up; but I begged of him to go ahead, and so he did. He obtained his charter, and the Company was then organized.

We had, perhaps, as respectable a body of directors as could be found in our whole city; and of that body I am the only remaining member.

A little later, as you have been told, I was President, subsequently and gladly giving place to my friend Bancker, a man to whose energy and honesty you are indebted for the wonderful success that you, Mr. President, have just now described. No man ever did give to any service more energy, more activity, more determination, more honesty than were given to his company by our departed friend. And I now ask you to join me in drinking to the memory of the late President, Charles N. Bancker, one of the best men our fair city has produced.

THE PRESIDENT: The next regular toast is

"OUR FRIENDS. WE BID THEM WELCOME; WE GREET THEM WITH OPEN HANDS; WE WISH THEM GOD SPEED!"

George W. Biddle, Esq., replied as follows:

GEORGE W. BIDDLE.

Mr. President and Gentlemen,—Were I to consult my own wishes on this occasion I should certainly be a silent participant in the festivities of this day. After what has been said, and so well said, so exhaustively said, in regard to the condition of the Company whose semi-centennial anniversary we celebrate, any words from me are words of supererogation. Yet, as the pleasing duty of responding to this toast has been imposed upon me, I must acquit myself of it as best I can.

When, a day or two ago, it was announced to me by the President that I was to reply to the toast just read, I began, under the influence of a custom which from professional habit has become almost inveterate, to try to analyze the meaning of the words which I was to answer,—" OUR FRIENDS !" The friends of a corporation! the friends of the Franklin Fire Insurance Company of Philadelphia! Can a soulless body, as a corporation is defined to be, have friends? The *President* has many friends who wish him well, and will long continue to do so. The *Officers* have friends. The only living ex-President who has honored us ¡with his presence to-day (Hon. Henry C. Carey) has many friends, among whom I may count myself among the humblest, certainly not the least, for I may say I have looked up to him from my earliest boyhood as the friend of my deceased parent, and as a citizen distinguished for his eminence in more than one walk in intellectual life.

But has a corporation friends? Yes, it has ; because upon the same basis that the friendship of individuals reposes may friendship be well asserted of a corporation like this. What are the sources of true friendship; not of the mere casual intimacy begot by interest, selfishness, or the like, but of true friendship? I take it, it is respect founded upon integrity, liberality, amenity of manners, and a certain sympathy of thought and action.

Now, if I can show to you, in the few words with

5

which I shall trouble you, that the Franklin Fire Insurance Company justly rests upon such a foundation as this, then. we may say that we are at least entitled to have friends. And when I look down the long line of sympathetic, cordial faces which grace this hospitable board, I may say we are not only *entitled to*, but we *have*, friends in the very best sense of the word. Have we endeavored to conduct our business upon the eternal principles of justice? Have we, in addition to mere cold, impartial justice, occasionally added the virtue of liberality? Have we shown kindness in our intercourse with our customers, and have we joined to it sympathy of manner? I think we have done all this. No company, let me say, Mr. President and gentlemen, can, in the course of half a century, have reached the magnificent —yea, the magnificent—financial results which you have declared to us to-day have been the meed of the Franklin Fire Insurance Company, without having conducted their affairs upon the sound basis of justice to their customers, and good sense and liberality in the administration of their business.

These results are not of chance. Chance may be for a year, for half a dozen years, but for half a century of unintermittent prosperity, which shows itself in the average of dividends of twenty per cent., it is impossible that it can repose upon any other basis than the basis of eternal truth in the administration of human affairs. This may be received as an axiom. There is no chance in this: dividends beginning a year or two after the inauguration of the Company, and ending with quarterly dividends of eight per cent., or thirty-two per cent. per annum, are the product of no chance. It is therefore justice; justice to the customers, justice to the stockholders.

Justice is a very good basis to repose upon, but it is not enough to bring about friendship. A man may be just but may be very disagreeable. He may discharge all his legal obligations, and may leave undischarged what lawyers call the duties of imperfect obligation,—the moral duties. He may be in form a good man, and yet be in substance a bad man. The height of justice is sometimes the height of injustice. In sticking too closely to the letter we very often smother and sometimes annihilate the spirit; and we have the highest warrant in saying this.

Has, therefore, the course of the Franklin Fire Insurance Company been governed by enlightened liberality as well as justice? I think, yes. I have now in my recollection one or two instances which I think you will bear with me whilst I state. When the great fire of 1845 swept almost out of existence our sister city of the West, Pittsburgh, a man had a temporary policy upon his building (not a dwelling-house, but a place of business), that had expired the day before. Justice required no payment on account of this policy, because it had ceased to be a contractual relation twenty-four hours before the calamity occurred, but enlightened liberality, enlightened selfishness if you please, dictated a different course, and that course was—as the man had intended *bona fide* to renew his policy, and was only prevented by some accident that I do not now recollect—that the policy should be paid, and it was paid in full. This is what I call liberality.

Another instance. The proprietor of a large manufacturing establishment, located at the Falls of Schuylkill, now embraced in the limits of the Park, fancied that he had a claim against the Franklin Fire Insurance Company for a larger sum than they were willing to pay. His claim say was for $10,000, and the Company thought they owed him but $5000. In strict law they were not obliged to pay anything until the courts should decide whether the smaller or the larger sum was the limit of their liability. But that would not have been honorable, or just. They knew they owed him so much, and they gave him a check for it, and said to him, "Now fight us for the rest, and get it if you can;" and, of course, the Company going into court and before a jury with such an advantage, went out of it triumphant.

That was right; that was moral; but it was not required by strict law; therefore I say we are liberal.

I might say a great deal about sympathy and amenity of manners; but really when I see looking into my face the delightfully sympathetic face of my respected and honored friend (the President), somewhat younger than I am, and when I look down at the other end of the table, and see the pleasant face of our still younger friend (the Vice-President), I need hardly say to you that this is a grace we claim to possess in a very high degree. I do not think *this* requires much further explanation. (Applause.)

I say, therefore, Mr. President and gentlemen, that resting as we do—as I think we do—upon such foundations, I may truly welcome you as friends. Indeed, I am an interested party in this; for (I may speak thus much of myself), of the fifty years of the existence of the Franklin Fire Insurance Company, every one of which my honored and venerable friend who sits near me (Mr. Carey) has seen, I myself, in a professional connection, have seen over thirty-three and a third years. My connection, it is true, began when I was a stripling at the Bar, in the year 1844; and here I am to-day, perhaps not quite so good as I was then, but still with some capacity for work in me, talking to you in 1879, —thirty-five years, more than two-thirds of the whole existence of the "Franklin."

We are therefore entitled—and I think I have read our title pretty clear—to say to you, *friends* in the best sense of the word; *friends* reposing upon our integrity, upon our liberality, upon our kindness of manner, upon our sympathies, Come to our hearts! You are not only "welcome to our hands," as I think the language of the toast reads, but to our hearts, too. Such friends as we see before us to-day are not to be received merely with the impress of the closed hand, but, as the poet says, "are to be grappled to our souls with hooks of steel," for their devotion has been proved. They are really friends. They have stood by us, as the late Vice-President, Mr. George Fales, and his estate have stood, from the first to the last. There has been no faltering; there has been no hesitation. When the skies were gloomy and the clouds were lowering, no thought of severing their interests from the interests of the Company which had stood by them entered their hearts; they remained faithful and firm. They are not holiday friends, not summer friends, but friends of a lifetime. Welcome to them!

But there are other friends; there are absent friends; there are friends separated from us by distance of time and space, some of whom have sent in their excuses to-day. There are others whose duty is finished forever upon earth, and whom we can only trace in the retrospect of memory.

I recollect TWO who shared the hospitalities of this Board with us just a decade ago. I find that on the 25th of June, 1869, just after your accession, Mr. President, to the chief executive office of this Company, we dined here, I think, in this very room; certainly on this very day, the 25th day of June, which we now learn was the date on which this Company began its active business. There were present then, with the other directors, two who were peculiarly dear to me, now no more: GEORGE W. RICHARDS, THOMAS SPARKS. One an eminently successful merchant, the other deserving eminent success, but not achieving it, or at least not retaining it.

I never met either of those gentlemen without a cordial smile and a gracious, kind remark, or something to indicate that it was more than the mere casual meeting of an acquaintance. We may not drink their health, but we may recall their memory in solemn silence. We may pause to recall the good example that they set before us in their lifetime, and we may hope that when we, too, go down to our resting-place—and many of us can no longer call ourselves young, or even middle-aged men—we may hope that we may be embalmed in the recollection of our fellows assembled here to-day. And if we do in our day and generation perform any good works, no matter how small, the odor of those works may come up as a sweet-smelling savor to those who ·remain, and cause a grateful recollection of us who have passed before them.

THE PRESIDENT: The third regular toast is as follows:

" IN MEMORY OF THE DEAD. THEIR ASSOCIATES IN THE DIREC-TORSHIP STILL LIVING PAY A TRIBUTE TO THEIR WORTH, AND MAKE A MINUTE IN THEIR HEARTS OF THE GOOD THEY DID WHEN ON EARTH. CHARLES N. BANCKER, SAMUEL GRANT, GEORGE W. RICHARDS, THOMAS SPARKS, AND GEORGE FALES. PASSED AWAY, BUT NOT FORGOTTEN."

Our associate director, Gustavus S. Benson, will reply to that toast.

GUSTAVUS S. BENSON.

Mr. President and Gentlemen,—The eloquent remarks that we have already heard with regard to our departed friends, both from the President and our Counsel, will make but a very few words necessary from me in answering to such a sentiment. But standing as we do in this semi-centennial year of our corporate existence, at the very pivotal point of our corporate century, looking back upon the past, looking forward to the future, I think it is well for us even on this festive occasion, even for a few moments, to dwell upon that future which will come to us all, and to which our friends have gone before,—to that bourne from which no traveller has ever returned.

These five gentlemen who are to be remembered to-day have been, at some period of life, either in intimate social or business relations with me. I have been acquainted with and had business intercourse with them all. Three of them lived beyond the extreme age of ninety years. In speaking of Mr. Bancker, we all know how he moulded the policy of this Company; how he controlled its business, and how great was his influence upon its prosperity; not only in his own day, but carrying it down to ours. The business talent, the undoubted integrity, the genial manners, of our late respected friend George Fales we never can forget.

In 1812 I was brought from a neighboring State to this city. Whether against my will or not I am unable now to say; I was of course at that time a lad. A very few years afterwards, in 1816, I found myself living next door to Samuel Grant, then a very young married man, in Market Street below Eleventh, opposite what was called Girard Row; the whole square now covered with stately stores and handsome mansions, in the care and management of which even at this day I have something to do. I can well recollect his youthful appearance by looking at his son, an honored member of this Board, whom we all love and all respect. From that circumstance, and knowing him from that time to the day of his death, I may say that his whole life lies before my mind; a life that this community holds to be without spot or blemish, leaving a name which is a rich inheritance to his children.

The genial spirits of our younger friends whom Mr. Biddle has spoken of,—Mr. Sparks and Mr. Richards,— always come to us with pleasant memories. We shall never forget the happy associations we have had with them in the Board and out of the Board. But when we look at the past, when we remember these men and what they were, and what they did, it seems to me that this Company has great cause to be proud of its past history; and while we are satisfied with the present, we may look forward with hope, feeling that its future career may be as successful as its past record is honorable. (Applause.)

THE PRESIDENT: The next toast in order is

"THE SENIOR AGENT OF THE FRANKLIN,"

James W. Cochran, who has travelled from Lexington, Kentucky, to sit with us to-day.

JAMES W. COCHRAN.

—*Mr. President and Gentlemen,*—It has been my good

fortune on several occasions to be present at this festive board. I have travelled many miles to be here, and there has never been a more interesting gathering than this very semi-centennial. Upon reading the kind invitation of the President my first feeling was that I could not come. After reading his letter further, on the importance of my being here, I made up my mind at once; and the consequence is I am now present.

The President has very kindly mentioned my name in connection with his history of the Company, and it leaves me but very little to say. He has gone over the whole ground; yet I feel I cannot let this moment pass without saying something of my own connection with the Company. As the President has said to you, when quite a youth I was employed by my old friend John Tilford as surveyor of the Company. I served in that capacity four years; after that time I was made agent of the Company. Since that date the Company has had a continuous agent in the city of Lexington for forty-eight years.

You will all recollect that in those forty-eight years we have gone through a rebellion. Notwithstanding the city of Lexington was for two months in a state of rebellion, under the control of some of the Southern Confederacy, the business of the " Franklin" was continued during that time, so far as the renewals on the books were concerned; not through any instructions given me by Mr. Bancker, but of my own volition. During the whole time there never was a dollar lost. (Applause.)

I take great pleasure in saying that during the whole forty-eight years of my services for the Company, I do not recollect of an unpleasant thing between the Company and myself, either under its old administration or under the present. Everything has been amicably done by us. I have thought sometimes they placed more confidence in me than they should do, for I have had the control of the business in my own section in my own hands. No company has stood higher in that locality than she has for justice, ability, and fairness. During the whole period that I have been agent we have never had but one lawsuit, and that was with a man who had been burned out three times; every one offered to compromise the matter and get rid of it, but he proved unreasonable and went to court. He had a bad lawyer; I think if he had had such counsel as Mr. Biddle he would have fared better. As it was, the jury gave him three hundred dollars less than I had offered him. That is the only legal contest in my local department of the Company.

I am happy to say that the Company stands just as high in the estimation of the community as she has ever done; and I am perfectly satisfied that the "Franklin" will be able to hold on to all the business she has ever had in that region. (Applause.)

THE PRESIDENT: I next call upon our esteemed agent at Pittsburgh, Mr. J. G. Coffin.

J. G. COFFIN.

Mr. President,—I had hoped, in the presence of so much learning and ability, you would have excused me from any remarks on this festive occasion. After your own eloquent address and the very interesting remarks, so felicitously expressed, by those who have preceded me, I could not say anything that would be found of interest, and would fain give place to others more suited to the task; but having noticed here, as almost every time I have been present at a meeting of underwriters, some things peculiar to the profession, I will mention one such. The Company whose guests we are has made an average dividend of twenty per cent. during its life of fifty years, and this fact is justly counted as one of the evidences of its success and able management; whilst on the opposite side of this festive board sits the honored representative of an older company, that has never made a dividend, and yet it too is esteemed one of eminent success. Who but an underwriter, or one somewhat acquainted with the profession, could understand this seeming anomaly? Thanking you for the honor of a seat at this board on this very pleasant occasion, and knowing my inability to add anything to the enjoyment or pleasure of this exceptionally able presence, I hope you will excuse me from any further remarks.

THE PRESIDENT : The next toast in order is

"'HOME,'—BEAUTIFUL WORD! THE COMPANY THAT BEARS SO FITTING A NAME HAS CELEBRATED HER FIRST QUARTER-

CENTURY. WE GREET HER WITH WORDS OF GOOD CHEER IN HER
ONWARD MARCH TO GREATER SUCCESS,"

which will be responded to by Mr. Charles J. Martin,
its President. (Applause.)

CHARLES J. MARTIN.

Mr. President,—If I had known when you sent me the
invitation to be present on this pleasant occasion that
I was to be called upon to make any speech, or to respond to a toast, I should have hesitated before accept-
ing it, and would probably have tried to transfer it to
the talking man of my Company, as I am "more a man
of deeds than of words." As you very well know your-
self, it is necessary for a Company to have connected
with it a man that can talk ; and our Second Vice-President, Mr. D. A. Heald, as you also very well know, is
the talkist of my Company. (Applause.)

I am very glad to be here to-night, notwithstanding.

You have made a pleasant reference to my connection
with your Company. I was its agent thirty years ago
in the city of New York; and you were pleased to read
the result of my agency during the time that I represented the "Franklin ;" and although the figures had
passed from my recollection, it is very satisfactory to
find them thus noted in your report this evening.

When I resigned the agency of the "Franklin" I re-
gretted it for certain reasons, with which you are par-
tially acquainted ; and if those reasons had not existed,
so that the relations might have continued, I cannot but

believe that the New York agency of the "Franklin" would have proved even a grander success. You made one little mistake in your report in regard to my sliding at once into the "Home," for there was an intervening period of three years before the "Home" was organized, during which I was the secretary of another company.

You have honored my Company with your toast. The "Home" has had its first quarter-century's career, and you, Mr. President, personally, as one of its shareholders, have a copy of the record, which shows satisfactory results, notwithstanding the heavy draft upon its resources by the two greatest conflagrations which have visited this continent.

I would say a word in regard to the "Home" and the "Franklin" which is of interest to both. The name of my Company had been adopted before I accepted the secretaryship, and when I saw it announced in the papers that there was to be a Home Insurance Company organized, I thought it was a singular name for a fire insurance company, and rather a tame one too. But I soon found it to be a very popular name, for Home Insurance Companies grew up, or tried to grow up, all over the country, some of them hoping to profit by the prestige the name had already gained in one instance; but ill success followed many of these attempts, and most of our namesakes have since gone into oblivion. I claim that there is but *one* "Home Insurance Company." And so it has been, and is, with your Company. The Franklin Insurance Company of Philadelphia is *the* Franklin Insurance Company of the country. We have had two in New York: one burned up in 1835 legitimately and honorably in the great fire of that year, and one commenced a few years since, and after a hard struggle has just gone out of existence; and I know there are many more of the same name elsewhere. I want to congratulate ourselves, however, that there can be but *one* "*Home*" and *one* "*Franklin*" in the true sense, believing that attempts to borrow the name of a successful institution as a prestige of success ought to fail, and will fail. (Applause.) –

I am very much gratified to meet you, Mr. President and gentlemen, and particularly to see and hear these venerable men, whose presence honors this company to-night, some of whom I have long known by reputation, and some I have met in years past. There is one thing that especially attracted my notice this evening: from the remarks made in connection with the history of the Company, it seems to have been a good thing for those who desire long life to be directors of the Franklin Fire Insurance Company, for of the departed ones referred to in your report I was particularly struck with the fact of the large proportion who had reached into the *eighties* and *nineties;* and then look at these octogenarians, or nearly so, who are left, and who support you on either hand! The younger members of your Board may thus look forward to the ripened years they may hope to reach, and to the duties and responsibilities of the next twenty-five or fifty years. And we will trust that they may bear the banner in the future as successfully as their elders have in the past, so that when the next quarter-century or "the *Centennial*" is celebrated they may be here filling these honored places.

And I am glad to meet my venerable friend over there on your right, Mr. Richard Smith, the venerable President of "The Union," whom I have not seen for twenty-five or thirty years, and who is now one of the veteran underwriters of the country.

Although so much the junior of many now in this room, I am one of the oldest fire underwriters. There is, I believe, but one now in the business who antedates me in the business of fire insurance in this country.

It would give me pleasure to say more if I thought I could interest you, but, as I said before, I am not a man of words so much as of deeds. (Applause.)

The President: We now pass back to 1752, and propose:

"The Philadelphia Contributionship."

It will be responded to by Jas. Somers Smith, Esq., its executive officer.

JAMES SOMERS SMITH.

Mr. President,—In rising to respond to that toast I have to remark, I am very sorry the arrangement was changed from what you originally intended, which was that the representative of that Company should remain seated. To be put upon my feet is, for me, to be placed in an unnatural position. I am here as the "Old Fogy," representing the *oldest* fire insurance company in America, and feel very much out of place when called upon to make a speech, for three reasons: first, I belong to the family of Smiths, who have the reputation of being extremely modest; then, they generally are not orators, although my uncle Richard S. Smith is a bright exception; and lastly, you have "a chiel amang ye takin' notes," and I fear he will "print them."

I was very much struck with one fact, brought out in the President's address, with reference to the origin of "The Franklin." Their first meeting took place at "Rubicam's," the best eating-house existing in Philadelphia fifty years ago,—and Mr. Dutilh will tell you there was never a better place to dine in this city; and all here agree with me in approving of the continuance of that custom.

I have been much enlightened by the information received here to-day, and am sorry I cannot impart wisdom to you myself. The Company I represent never had an agent, and when I look around me and see all these gentlemen who have contributed to the success of the "Franklin," I feel I ought to have stayed away. I have been connected with insurance since 1853. A better man for the business never existed than the late Charles N. Bancker. He was the father of insurance by agents, and was the originator of many matters beneficial to its interests, and which have resulted, as Mr. Baker has shown us, in the Company's paying most excellent dividends. The Company I represent has never paid a cent in that way. They are purely mutual, for the perpetual insurance of brick or stone buildings in Philadelphia. They started with names of eminent citizens as signers of their Deed of Settlement, among whom was Benjamin Franklin, who was the first elected director. They placed badges of four hands on all buildings insured. In those days fires were extinguished with leather fire-buckets and small hand-engines; and as trees in front of houses interfered with application of water, the Company charged an additional deposit for each tree. More than thirty years afterwards—in 1784—The Mutual Assurance Company commenced business, and not objecting to trees, the badge adopted by them was a green tree.

In conclusion, I would remark that representing a Company that is one hundred and twenty-seven years old, I am delighted to see the success that has attended the one now celebrating its semi-centennial.

THE PRESIDENT: The next toast would have been responded to by David Lewis, Secretary and Treasurer,

"THE MUTUAL ASSURANCE OF 1783."

In his absence I have brought to this gathering a policy, which I own, issued by the " Green Tree."

The " Green Tree " took its name, I believe, because the old Hand-in-Hand, which Mr. Smith represents, were such old fogies they would not insure a house with any trees around it, because they attracted the lightning; and also because water could not be thrown over the trees and put out the fire with the hand-engines then in use. Therefore in 1784 competition came in, and the Mutual Assurance Company was started to be more liberal in its policy. The name of "Green Tree" attached to the Company from the above reasons, and it still continues to be so known.

This policy was written in the year 1804, February 15, No. 1765. It is very different from the policies of the present day, for it has only one condition: "*Provided, and it is hereby declared, that this policy shall not take effect or be binding if the said house, &c.*, *be now or hereafter insured in any other office, unless the same shall be allowed of by the trustees of this office, and specified on the back of this policy.*" That was independence! They would have no competition in those days. I do not know whether they would allow the Philadelphia Contributionship to be on a risk with them as co-insurers.

There is another singular thing about this old policy. It is issued to "Philip Odenheimer, on a two-story dwelling-house, on the south side of Sassafras Street, between Fourth and Fifth, as per survey No. 725. On the house, $700; on the back building, $700; stables and slaughter-house, $600. Total, $2000 at 3½ per cent. Policy and incidental expenses, $6." That is ahead of modern charges.

The next date we arrive at is 1794. In that year two prominent Philadelphia companies had their birth; there is some doubt which was born first in that year. As Mr. Platt has sent us his toast, accompanying his regret, and as Mr. H. D. Sherrerd used to be connected with the Insurance Company of North America in an official capacity, it is to be hoped he will respond for both. These two companies are the Insurance Company of the State of Pennsylvania and the Insurance Company of North America, both organized in 1794. Mr. Henry D. Sherrerd, a relic of the last century,——

MR. BIDDLE.

Which is the relic, the Company or Mr. Sherrerd?

HENRY D. SHERRERD.

I apprehend our friend has but one meaning; every one can understand that.

Mr. President and Gentlemen,—Speaking is not in my line. (Laughter.) You may laugh as much as you please, but that is a fact; it is a truism that cannot be controverted. (Laughter.) I am in this fix, and when I look back a period of fifty years that this magnificent Franklin Company has been in existence, it is sublime to think of it through all the trials and incidents of that half-century; that we see it here to-day in such a state of prosperity that we can predicate from its past history that another fifty years it will be entirely out of sight. I mean to say their prosperity will be so great in that time that all then living will be congratulating them, as we now do.

From 1682—the year that our city was founded, surveyed, and regulated—until 1752, a period of seventy years, there does not appear to have been an Incorporation having for its object the business of protecting the community from losses consequent upon the ravages of fire. During that long period there were private Insurers, or Underwriters, who underwrote marine hazards, but the people were apparently satisfied to run their own fire risks. The incorporation of the Philadelphia Contributionship (Hand-in-Hand), in 1752, was the first effort to introduce into the city what of late years has been so essential for protection and indemnification from losses by fire. At that time, the population was estimated to be about 20,000. In 1784, The Mutual Assurance (Green Tree) Company was incorporated, the first rival and only competitor of the Contributionship. These two Companies had the field to themselves until 1794, when the Insurance Company of North America and the Insurance Company of the State of Pennsylvania were incorporated, the former with a capital of $600,000 and the latter with a capital of $500,000. Both Companies were privileged to transact a Fire, Marine, and Inland Transportation business. The two corporations doing business prior to 1794 were organized on the mutual plan, while those two which commenced to issue policies in that year were stock corporations. We will skip over a period of forty-three years, and in 1837 we find seventeen local companies in good standing, transacting the insurance business:

Marine and Fire	2
Marine exclusively	7
Perpetual Fire	2
Fire exclusively	6
	—17

Among the latter, the name of the Franklin occupies an honored place for reliability. Permit me to say, that in this year of grace we have more insurance capital and assets in this goodly city of Brotherly Love than is requisite for its wants, viz.:

	Capital.	Assets.
29 Local companies . . .	$7,333,100	$28,992,719.43
In addition to these there are 139 agencies of companies located outside the city		84,272,851.00
Showing aggregate of assets .		$113,265,570.43

Mr. President, if you will allow me, I will speak of some of the peculiarities of the insurance business in Philadelphia.

I have stated elsewhere that insurance was without music or poetry, a proposition to which I have no doubt you will agree with me. Nevertheless, I am in possession of a bill of lading with an old Dutch galiot for a vignette, which reads, "Shipped by the Grace of God by Geo. Fox and James Thomas, of Philadelphia, on board the good ship 'Marmaid' [it is to be presumed that she was a sloop] four boxes of soape bound to Barbadoes," terminating with the pious hope, " and so God send the good ship to her desired port in safety, bearing date ye 9th mo., 9th, 1696," one hundred and eighty-two years ago. A peculiarity of this bill of lading is that it is signed by " Robert Grymes," the master. The fame of this good old man has been celebrated in song and story as long back as the memory of man runneth; and it is satisfactory to know that he pursued the respectable though perilous calling of an ancient mariner. So you will perceive that there is some connection between marine insurance and both music and poetry.

Now, Mr. President, I have nothing further to say except to express the wish that in the future the prosperity of the Company may, if possible, exceed the past, and that its Officers and Directors may always serve it with integrity and fidelity in years to come as they have in those gone by.

THE PRESIDENT: The toast next in order is,

"THE UNION, OF PHILADELPHIA, 1804."

To be responded to by Richard S. Smith, its President; and I wish to remark that I esteem it a great compliment that a gentleman who will be ninety years of age if he lives until next August is now with us to-day, and graces our table. (Applause.)

RICHARD S. SMITH.

Gentlemen,—I cannot say much, except that I do feel proud to be so kindly noticed by this Company. I have nothing to say worthy your attention, except, perhaps, some experiences of my early youth.

One of the gentlemen has mentioned having been present at the funeral procession of General Washington. I was also there, and that before I was twenty-one years of age, when I was sent abroad with a ship and cargo worth a hundred thousand dollars. There were many things connected with that passage that were quite interesting. There was danger of our vessel being captured, and I had to discharge her cargo in Gottenberg in Sweden. We had no consul there, and although the youngest man among them, they elected me consul. I presume it was because I had been wise enough to go into a Swedish family and had acquired the language in one year. It was of no pecuniary advantage to me, but it took me into all the best society. Every vessel that came into port had to present her papers to me as consul. As the quarantine was in practice at that time, I received the papers of the schooner "Champion," which had cleared from New York to Eastport, Maine. I had, when Madison's message was delivered, in 1811, written a letter to my father in which that message was very severely criticised, as he ignored all the wrongs we were suffering from France ; for I had examples of our vessels being caught out by French cruisers, which were condemned without giving them any chance at all. President Madison never dwelt upon this fact in any way.

I imagined when this vessel came in there that war had been declared, for here was a small vessel which had cleared for Eastport, Maine, in a Swedish port. Therefore, I got a boat, took my consular certificate along with me, went down from the wharf, and the quarantine master passed it up to the captain. I said, " Captain, what brought you here ?" He said, " I came out on a confidential errand, and I cannot talk about it." I supposed he did not want to talk before the old

Swede. I asked him to let me put him on a rock, and I rowed the boat out myself alongside, and then said to him, " Now, captain, if you have some more important information which affects the interests of your owners, remember that other Americans have the same interest to defend, and I think you ought to let me know it." He said, " I tell you I cannot talk." I said, " Do you see that convoy that lays there,—an English convoy, waiting for a wind? There are thirty or forty sail of your country in that convoy, and, if I comprehend the state of affairs, the admiral will capture every one within four and twenty hours." He then said war had been declared on the 18th of June.

I hastened up to town and called the Americans together. Many were the captains of these vessels, and they were scared out of their wits. However, they wrote circulars which were taken down and distributed among these ships, and before daylight they were under the Swedish batteries, and there was a great inquiry as to what had got into the Yankees.

Soon after that I started to go home, and had to go by the way of England. When I arrived in London I heard of the capture of General Hull and his American army that had surrendered in Canada. After my return home I did not go into business until 1815. In 1830 I was elected a Director of the Union Insurance Company, where I have been ever since; it will be fifty years next January. Then I was elected President in 1837, so that my insurance experience has been a pretty long one.

8

I do not know that I have much more to say, except that I am a pretty old fellow. (Applause.)

THE PRESIDENT: " The American Fire Insurance Company, 1810." Mr. Thomas R. Maris sent his regrets.

"The Fire Association, 1820." Mr. A. Loudon Snowden sent an acceptance, but for some unknown reason is not present.*

"The Pennsylvania Fire Insurance Company, 1825." A regret was also received from its President, Mr. John Devereux.

A very modest gentleman is on my left. He is not a man of words; he has held a very responsible position in Philadelphia for very many years as President of the Pennsylvania Life and Annuity Company. I propose the health of Charles Dutilh, who was secretary of the first meeting held by the stockholders of the Franklin Fire Insurance Company.

CHARLES DUTILH.

I am very thankful to you, gentlemen, for drinking to my health, but being no speaker you must excuse me from making any remarks.

THE PRESIDENT: I see sitting down at the end of the table a gentleman that I am associated with in another walk of life,—in a board of directors in which he is my president, viz., Commercial National Bank. I wish to

---

* Sudden indisposition kept Mr. Snowden absent.

say that Mr. Claghorn has done a great deal for the city of Philadelphia in many ways, but especially as the patron of art. I give as a toast

"THE AMERICAN ACADEMY OF FINE ARTS: ITS PRESIDENT, JAMES L. CLAGHORN."

JAMES L. CLAGHORN.

Gentlemen,—I only rise to acknowledge the compliment paid me by the President in his reference to my connection with the Academy of Fine Arts. This is the second occasion on which he has chosen to refer to me in connection with art, and I acknowledge it in this brief manner, as I am a man of deeds rather than words. As a large portion of my life has been devoted to business, I have of course come much in contact with insurance companies; and with three of the older companies,—the Franklin, Insurance Company of North America, and Green Tree,—which I have known almost from childhood, my associations have been very close with them and their officers.

HENRY C. CAREY.

I propose, as a fitting tribute, that we now drink the health of the Vice-President of the Company, James W. McAllister.

JAMES W. McALLISTER.

Mr. President and Gentlemen,—I thank you for the compliment tendered, and express much inward gratification that the venerable ex-President, Mr. Carey, should have offered so courteous a toast. Two days hence I will have completed my twenty-sixth year of service in this institution. On the 27th of June, 1853, I commenced my duties as a subordinate clerk. Since that time the changes have been varied and great in truth, as my mind recalls the doings of more than a quarter of a century. Mr. Baker has so thoroughly covered the history of the corporation it leaves me but little to say, unless I refer to the changes that have taken place within my memory.

Of all the members of the Board of Directors in office in 1853 but one, Mr. Isaac Lea, remains. All the officers I found there have passed away; an entirely new set of men have taken their places. During this time, however, the corporation has remained the same as regards its reliability and prominence. The methods of doing business have entirely changed; in fact, were it possible for some of the old officers to come back, they would hardly know how to proceed. The men and the times have changed, the fire hazard is greater, the system of putting out fires has changed, as also the ways of setting places on fire have increased very materially. The only two persons I can call to mind, except Mr. Lea, in connection with the Franklin in 1853, and who are still with us, are the counsel of the Company, Messrs. Eli K. Price and George W. Biddle. From early youth to manhood, therefore, my life, in its every-day duties, has been linked in closest ties with this Company; and as I look back over the many changes that I have seen in my time, how little did I think, over twenty-five years ago, that a day would come when I should be called to fill the chair once occupied by my steadfast friend, my honored predecessor, George Fales!

THE PRESIDENT: I now call upon one of the directors to respond to the toast,

"THE MERCANTILE INTERESTS OF THE CITY OF PHILADELPHIA:"

Colonel R. Dale Benson.

R. DALE BENSON.

Mr. President,—I was complimented by you in being a member of the committee of arrangements in the celebration of the semi-centennial of the Franklin Fire Insurance Company, but I do not remember of anything being said about my being called upon to respond to any toast. I will, however, say a few words in response to the sentiment.

It has given me a great deal of pleasure to listen to the reminiscences of the last half-century, and I must confess to the feeling of being somewhat appalled with a sense of the responsibility which must rest upon the rising generation. And representing that element in the Franklin directorship, I can only say it is our duty to do all we can to continue the same conservative course in future years as has marked its past career.

In responding to "The Mercantile Interests of Philadelphia," as a young representative of the merchants of this great city, I take great pleasure in stating that I believe as a class they have no superior in their conservative methods of doing business and in the matter of their credit in the marts of the world, and it may be well questioned whether they have been surpassed anywhere for energy of character. In these respects it is to be doubted whether they are outranked in America or in the Old World.

How closely allied the mercantile and insurance interests are it would be needless to argue in this presence, nor is it necessary to say that the mercantile interests have found the necessity of availing themselves of the protection of the insurance companies. You are all familiar with the details of these facts. The merchants of Philadelphia patronize to a very large extent the companies of our own city. They have been taught by experience to feel confidence in and put their trust in them.

THE PRESIDENT: I have a toast here to

"THE LOSS DEPARTMENT,—A NECESSARY EVIL. THE LESS IT HAS TO DO THE MORE THE PROFIT,"

and call upon General Agent Blodget to respond.

AMOS C. BLODGET.

Mr. President,—If I understand the toast, the Loss Department is a necessary evil. I do not see it. Insurance companies were organized to pay losses, and the loss department cannot therefore be a necessary evil. Those who have addressed you here to-night, older in

experience than I am, tell you that it is one of the bright-
est jewels in the crown of an insurance company that it
has been able, from its organization, through its entire
existence, to meet justly and equitably the demands
made upon its treasury. That the man himself at the
head of the loss department may be a necessary evil, or
an evil of some kind, may be a debatable question, but if
the loss department is a necessary evil it is also a necessary requisite, and I submit that proposition to every-
body who holds a policy of insurance. Properly man-
aged, indeed, all the leading companies of the land
to-day, without exception, find it necessary, not only
from the magnitude of their business, to have a loss
department, but find it necessary to have at the head of
it a necessary evil.

I see Mr. Martin smile. I know it is no new experi-
ment with his company or with many others. It is not
an evil. We must have an organization to pay losses;
and to pay dividends, if we can. I have heard here to-
night, for the first time in my life, that companies have
been organized not to pay dividends. I suppose such
companies are purely mutual; but they must have of
necessity a loss department, and they do not consider it
a necessary evil. Let somebody move to strike out that
" it is a necessary evil" so as to give me an opportunity
to talk about the loss department. It is hard to talk as
it stands.

I will not, however, detain you upon a dry subject at
this late hour. I have nothing to say that would interest

you, and it would not certainly interest me. To consider losses is my daily duty, a subject that would be devoid of interest at such an hour and to such a gathering. The proceedings of this evening have greatly impressed me, for I have learned much from the President's address of which hitherto I was ignorant.

THE PRESIDENT: We have a new-comer to our board, the latest member. I have been puzzled to know what toast to give him. Turning it over in my mind, and knowing that he is able to speak for himself on all occasions, and to write his mind clearly, it has seemed very proper that he should respond to the toast of

"WOMAN."

My friend Derr, if I offer that toast and ask you to stand up and say a few words in favor of "Woman," will you do it? Therefore, gentlemen, we will say "Woman," to be responded to by Thompson Derr, of Wilkesbarre.

THOMPSON DERR.

Mr. President and Gentlemen,—The subject of the toast to which I am called to respond should have been delegated to our worthy President, as a party whom I have heard discuss it in his most eloquent style on a former occasion. Women, our mothers and sisters, your wives and daughters, of whom we should all be proud as the conservators of our morals; whose beauty in youth is admired by all, and whose advice in old age is a means of doing good beyond the calculation of the most sanguine. Who can look upon a pure woman except to revere her as the climax of the work carried out by Him who created all that is good?

THE PRESIDENT: There was placed before me during the progress of the dinner a very handsome floral tribute. It came very unexpectedly. I knew nothing of it. It bears the card, "Compliments of the Clerks of the Franklin," and the name, " Franklin, 1829–1879," very beautifully worked in raised flowers. Such a compliment has touched me nearly. While the employees of this Company have also enjoyed themselves in an adjoining room, this unlooked-for testimonial marked their kind intents. I accept these flowers as the typical emblem of their feeling this very day towards their President. It is beautiful in its character, and I have felt in a double sense, as my eye has continuously fallen on those flowers, that there is something, as Mr. Biddle has very truthfully remarked, in friendship over and above the cold business relations of every-day life. It will ever be a green spot in my memory to think that the clerks thus kindly remembered the man that was the head executive of the Institution that furnished them and their families their livelihood.

Gentlemen, it is something to think that independent of a corporation being a copartnership merely to make money for its stockholders, it furnishes a livelihood; it gives bread and butter to hundreds of those who are connected with it in its various ramifications. There is no gentleman at this table who can appreciate that idea better to-day than the President of the Home Insurance Company. These are not words of flattery. During a visit to New York City a couple of weeks ago, Mr. Martin asked me if I would lunch with the officers about one o'clock in their new and beautiful quarters in the Boreel Building on Broadway. We were taken in an elevator up six stories, where the inner man of all their employees is looked after during office-hours. The officers had their special dining-room, while the clerks had their own particular apartment also. They had their own small tables, came up in corps or detachments, and when their time ended another set came up with military precision.

Our office is not probably as large as that, although within the building we have some thirty souls, officers and employees, attending every day to their appointed work. We are all component parts of a great community, and to the credit of no single man is to be placed the success of the corporation. I repeat, this is a beautiful tribute, and something never to be forgotten.

HENRY D. SHERRERD.

I propose the health and continued prosperity of the Company, and those who are represented by this beautiful dish of flowers.

GUSTAVUS S. BENSON.

Like my friend Sherrerd, I am no talkist. (Laughter.) I would have come even if I had known I was to have been called on to talk. What I rise to say is, it is very rarely in nature that a fact is produced without a cause. If we hear of an earthquake we are pretty well assured that away down in the bowels of the earth there are forces and moving principles that cause the great upheaval which we call an earthquake.

Our President says this beautiful testimonial touched him nearly; it touched me quite. I think it was an evidence of a very just appreciation of what is a very prominent characteristic of the President of this Company. I believe I have noticed it ever since I have been in the office, that where a man does his duty promptly, efficiently, industriously, there is not a man on earth that he could more safely trust with his friendship than the President of the "Franklin." I say nothing about the abilities of our chief officer, for we all know them. But there is an undercurrent to all this, a sentiment of good feeling that these clerks have. It is that that has prompted them to make this testimonial to-night, and I therefore propose a health to President Baker, with glasses full to the brim.

THE PRESIDENT.

Gentlemen,—In responding to both Mr. Sherrerd's and Mr. Benson's kind words, it must be known to all I have been talking a great deal this evening, and I will remark that there is an old saying that "*on their own merits modest men are dumb.*" When you all rise from your seats to drink my health, all that which is within me naturally responds to the compliment tendered.

I am now entering, as you well know, the second decade of my services as President of this Company. Where we will be, how many of us will sit around the Franklin table at its sixtieth anniversary, no man can tell,—no living being can even conjecture. The youngest is sometimes taken first. This is not a time to be sad ; it is the moment of mirth and congratulation. Thanking you for what you have said and done, and responding to all of your courtesies so freely offered, I can only borrow in conclusion words from Longfellow's most beautiful " Psalm of Life :"

> " NOT ENJOYMENT AND NOT SORROW
>   IS OUR DESTINED END OR WAY ;
> BUT TO ACT THAT EACH TO-MORROW
>   FINDS US FARTHER THAN TO-DAY."   (Applause.)

DINNER OF THE CLERKS.

In response to an invitation of the President and Board of Directors, the clerks met together in an adjacent room at Augustin's the same day at five o'clock. The full force was present, without exception. JOSEPH W. FLICKWIR occupied the chair. Shortly after being seated, the floral tribute, which had been prepared under the supervision of a committee, was submitted for inspection, unanimously approved as appropriate and emblematic, and sent in to the President with a neat card bearing the inscription, " Compliments of the Clerks of the Franklin."

Formal speech-making was not indulged in. Several toasts were, however, offered, which were received with the honor they merited, viz.,—

" THE HEALTH OF THE PRESIDENT AND BOARD OF DIRECTORS,"

and

"SUCCESS FOREVER TO THE OLD FRANKLIN."

Several stories, full of humor, and numerous anecdotes were the source of much merriment.

When the hour to part came, every one felt that the gathering had been a happy one, and that a few delightful hours had been passed in commemorating the " Golden Anniversary of the Old Franklin."

" WHEN LIFE IS OLD, AND MANY A SCENE FORGOT,
THE HEART WILL HOLD ITS MEMORY OF THIS HOUR."

www.ingramcontent.com/pod-product-compliance
Lightning Source LLC
Chambersburg PA
CBHW020251090426
42735CB00010B/1885